Bill Gates

Shashi Ambaru

AF517497

Prodigy

Bill Gates
New Horizon Media ©

First Edition: September 2008
64 Pages
Printed in India.

ISBN 978–81–8368–944–1
Pro–ya–en–25

Prodigy Books
177/103, First Floor, Ambal's Building,
Lloyds Road,Royapettah, Chennai 600 014.
Ph: +91-44-4200-9603

Email : support@nhm.in | Website : www.nhm.in

Prodigy Books is an imprint of New Horizon Media Private Limited

A Microsoft World

It was eight in the morning when the young man arrived at the office. He had a lot of work to do that day. He knew that he had some time alone before the office was filled with the noise of computers, telephones and people. Taking a cold glass of water from the filter, he slid into his chair and relaxed. The traffic was getting worse day by day. He was glad he had come ahead of his usual time. Otherwise, the morning rush hour traffic would have delayed him from starting work early. Taking a deep breath, he switched on his computer. A blue screen lit up and soon the Microsoft Windows logo appeared. The software engineer's day had begun.

A couple of hours later, in a different city, it was peak time at a small Internet centre. The place was full of students browsing the Net, mailing friends and printing resumés.

Two girls entered the café and made their way to the last computer. A man was busy working on the computer while another was supervising his work. The man looked up from his work at the girls. One of the girls took out her resumé from her bag and gave it to him. He nodded and said, 'Let me finish typing this man's work. Once I finish it, I'll start with yours. Can you come back in an hour?' The girl agreed and left. As he typed in the next word, the Auto Spell Check prompted him to correct the spelling. Silently thanking the efficient tools in Microsoft Word, he continued his work. Sometime later, when the document had been checked and re-checked, he finally saved it and began working on the girl's resumé.

Meanwhile, in a major university, it was a normal day of classes, lectures and seminars. All the Botany majors were getting prepared to attend their weekly student seminars. As they streamed inside the hall, one student stood away from the crowd. He smiled nervously as his classmates wished him luck for his seminar. He always had a fear of speaking before a crowd. But he was fully prepared. Thankfully, the seminar rules required him to use Microsoft Power Point. That made his job easier. Half of his points would be made by a sequence of visuals. Soon, he heard his name being announced. Standing at the podium, he started his seminar hesitantly.

By the time he played the first slide, his fears had disappeared and he continued confidently.

Miles away, a woman was busy completing her chores for the morning at home. Her husband sat in the porch reading his newspaper. He observed his wife hurriedly cooking their breakfast. It amused him slightly as he knew the reason for his wife's haste. He had retired a long time ago. His only son worked in the United States. It was only at night that his son's family had some free time. Owing to the time difference, it was morning in India when they could talk to their son. It was amazing how his wife had picked up the basics of the Internet when their grandson was born. Now, almost everyday, she logged on in MSN Messenger. Internet was the only medium that enabled her to talk to and see her son's family. The old man resumed his reading. But he soon heard his wife calling, 'Breakfast is ready. If you don't mind, you can continue your reading later."

'You know, I have other things to do.' Putting his paper down, the man went in, smiling to himself. It was late afternoon. Two schoolboys were returning home. They seemed to be having an excited discussion. One of them suddenly stopped and said, 'Yesterday, my father and I went to a digital showroom. Do you know what I saw in the display there? Xbox 360!'

The other widened his eyes and exclaimed, 'How was

it? Did you have a look at it?' The first boy replied, 'No, my father was in a hurry. So I couldn't spend much time there.' Both the boys sighed.

After a moment, they continued the conversation on their favourite topic, games.

The long day had finally come to an end for the software engineer. He stretched his tired arms and looked at his watch. It was time to go home. Before shutting down the computer, he took a look at the news. As he read the headlines in the international section, he checked the date on the calendar. It was 27 June 2008. He nodded his head as he read the story on the last day at work at Microsoft for its Chairman, Bill Gates.

Everyday, millions of people, from software engineers and school children to housewives and businessmen, make use of the computing tools developed by Microsoft. It is the software pioneer whose products include Microsoft Word, Power Point and Xbox, and a whole lot of technological innovations. Microsoft was the brainchild of Bill Gates who founded it along with Paul Allen, when barely out of school. With his vision and genius, Gates made Microsoft the software giant it is today. Though he has stepped down from his executive duties in the company, Bill Gates still remains one of the most recognisable icons of the software industry.

A Tryst with Destiny

The clanging of the school bell was lost in the din made by the Class VIII students. Once their Social Sciences teacher entered the classroom, they were all back at their places. She announced that they had to prepare a project on Bill Gates. She asked the class, 'Does anyone know anything about him?' Several hands went up. One boy said, 'Bill Gates is the richest man in the world.' The teacher smiled and asked another student. 'He's a software industrialist.' The teacher then had to listen to most of the students who had varied knowledge of who Bill Gates was and what he did. The teacher thought to herself, 'No matter how right or wrong my students are, I'm now sure there is hardly anyone who has not heard of Bill Gates!'

Bill Gates's fame has spread far and wide, thanks to his great success, business acumen and philanthropic work. His potential was evident right from his childhood. Born on 28 October 1955 in Seattle, Washington, in the United States, Gates belonged to a family of achievers. His father, William H Gates Sr, was a distinguished lawyer. His mother, Mary Maxwell Gates, was a school teacher. She also served as a chairperson on the board of United Way, a non-profit organisation. His ancestors held prominent positions in politics and business. His maternal grandfather, J W Maxwell, was the vice-president of a national bank. One of his great-grandfathers was a state legislator and mayor.

Gates was one of three children. He had an elder sister, Kristianne, and a younger one, Libby. He was known as William Gates III, though he was the fourth person in his family with that name. His father had dropped the suffix. Right from his early years in elementary school, Gates showed promise. He was exceptional in his studies, excellent in all the subjects. His parents planned a career in law for him. Sensing his remarkable intellect, they decided to enroll him in a premier school, Lakeside, a private and exclusive preparatory school, known for its academic environment.

Joining Lakeside proved to be an important step in his life. It was here that he became acquainted with the world of computers. Among his seniors was Paul Allen, with whom he would later begin a long-standing partnership.

In 1968, when Gates was in the eighth grade, the school decided to introduce computers to its students. At that time, computers were still bulky and very expensive to own. They were placed in huge, box-like frames. We call them mainframe computers. As these computers required specified conditions of temperature and electrical power, they were used only by large organisations.

In the 1960s and 70s, the concept of time sharing was extremely popular. Time sharing refers to the usage of a single computer by multiple users. They were priced so high that individual persons or even firms could not afford to buy or use them exclusively. So, people shared computers by using them in separate blocks of time. The school bought time on a computer owned by General Electric.

Bill Gates was often found glued to the computer along with Paul Allen and a couple of other students. Impressed by his interest in programming, the school allowed him to skip maths classes. He tried to program the system in BASIC (Beginner's All-purpose Symbolic Instruction Code), a high-level programming language. He designed an interactive program that allowed users to play the game tic-tac-toe with the computer. Their fascination for computers brought Allen and Gates together despite the two-year difference between them.

Their constant usage of the computer created some problems. They often missed classes and became slack in completing school work. Soon, the school found out that they had also managed to exhaust all the computer time the school had bought.

Fortunately, the parent of one of the Lakeside students worked in the Computer Center Corporation. The company had started operations in Seattle in the same year. It offered computer time at reasonable prices. This led to an agreement between the school and the company. Gates and his friends again had the chance to hone their skills on a new computer.

Though they developed their computer expertise, the members of the group got into trouble with the Computer Center Corporation. Finding loopholes in the computer's security system, they devised a way to acquire more computer time than the school had paid for. This led to frequent system crashes and they were finally caught. The company banned Gates and his friends, Allen, Ric Weiland, and Kent Evans, from using the computer.

Bill Gates and his friends started the Lakeside Programmers Group, very keen on continuing to work on computers. Ironically, the very company that banned them gave them a chance to do so.

In late 1968, the Computer Center Corporation faced several problems with its faulty security system. Believing the skills of the students could be useful, the company engaged the group to find the 'bugs' that weakened the security system, promising the boys additional computer time in exchange for their efforts. Thus, Gates and his group of computer enthusiasts had their wish granted. The time that Gates and Allen spent here proved to be crucial in determining their future. In fact, Gates once said, 'It was when we got free time at C-cubed (Computer Center Corporation) that we really got into computers. I mean, then I became hardcore. It was day and night.'[1]

Though the group's job was to detect bugs, they also got to spend a lot of time going through other computer-related information. They would continue working for CCC till March 1970, when financial problems forced the company to shut down. Gates and his friends now had no access to computers, but they were determined to find another source for obtaining computer time. Luckily for them, Allen's father worked in the University of Washington. They could spend their time and skills on a few computers on the campus. Soon, they would get another chance to exploit their potential.

In 1971, the Lakeside Programmers Group had another

lucky break. Information Sciences Inc. presented them with an opportunity to work on programming. They were asked to write a payroll program in COBOL (COmmon Business-Oriented Language). A payroll is a list of employees receiving wages or salaries, with the amounts due to each. The group would not only get computer time but also get royalties. This meant that whenever the company would make use of their programs, the group would be paid a share of the profit made. Thus, for the first time, the group's skills brought them money.

The school authorities were impressed by Gates's talent. He often wrote programs for the school for the organisation of class schedules. Allen used to help him out with the work. Soon, Allen and he decided to start their own company. As a result, in 1972, they began their new venture and named it Traf-O-Data. Gates was only seventeen at that time, and Allen was studying at Washington State University. They decided to develop programs on traffic usage from data produced by traffic counters, which measured the flow of road traffic.

The boys had the expertise to write programs, but they had no idea about designing hardware. So, they included another friend, Paul Gilbert, in the venture. Gilbert was given the responsibility to construct a computer. The three of them developed a computer that produced reports on traffic data. Their company had moderate success. It was closed when Gates left for college. However, the work they had done would help them eventually in beginning their next enterprise.

In late 1973, Gates was enrolled in college. He had scored 1590 out of 1600 in the SAT (Scholastic Aptitude Test and Scholastic Assessment Test) exams for admission into colleges in the United States. Gates won admission into Harvard College, the undergraduate section of Harvard University. Though he took the regular freshman courses and performed well in all of them, he was not interested in studies. He was most of the time found in the computer centre. Gates and Allen maintained contact throughout. They had dreams of setting up a new business. Both had a passion for software and had several ideas in mind. Allen was keen on starting a software company. But dropping out of college was a decision that Gates had to make. As he toyed with the idea of leaving college, he asked Allen to move close to Harvard. That would allow them to be in constant touch and plan their future course of action.

They worked together at the computer firm Honeywell in the summer. During that time, Gates began thinking about Allen's proposal. His parents knew his passion for computers and software. In spite of wanting a law career for him, they were supportive of any decision he would make. Before long, he made up his mind. His decision not only shaped his future but made history in the world of software technology.

An Era Begins

In 1975, two years after joining one of the most prestigious universities in the United States, Bill Gates dropped out of college. It was a remarkable decision made by a genius who knew there was a higher goal for him to achieve. What prompted him to do so was an interesting incident that also directly led to the birth of Microsoft.

The journey of Gates and Allen in the software industry began because of a magazine cover. Allen who went to meet Gates at Harvard came across the January 1st issue of *Popular Electronics* which featured the Altair 8800 with the headline 'World's First Minicomputer Kit to Rival Commercial Models'.

A microcomputer is a computer with a single microprocessor that serves as its central processing unit (CPU). It differed from a minicomputer whose CPU had several components. The microprocessor replaced the various circuits with a single Integrated Circuit (IC), commonly called chip. Thus, the microcomputer was smaller in size and therefore, occupied much less space than mainframe computers. When combined with a screen and a keyboard, it could be used as a personal computer.

Allen brought the magazine and showed it to Gates. Both of them knew that the Altair 8800 would revolutionise the computer market. They also realised the immense potential for software programming if microcomputers were successful. It was an opportunity they could not let go. Gates soon contacted Micro Instrumentation and Telemetry Systems (MITS), the company manufacturing the Altair. Gates informed them that he had developed software that could work on the Altair, though in reality, Allen and he had nothing ready. To their surprise, MITS expressed an interest to see the BASIC interpreter that Gates claimed to have written. (An interpreter is a computer program that executes the instructions written in a programming language).

Gates and Allen had not expected such an immediate reaction. They had not developed any interpreter. They did not own an Altair. They had to devote their time and energy to creating a BASIC interpreter that would work on the Altair 8800. They had to write software for a device they had no knowledge of. This was where their experience in Traf-O-Data helped them.

Allen had to test the software they now developed. He had access to the IBM 360 computers in his University. So he wrote a program on the IBM that would simulate the microprocessor in the computer they were designing. In a similar process, Allen tried to find a way to simulate Altair 8800 on the PDP-10 (a minicomputer named Programmed Data Processor) in the college. Gates took up the job of writing the software. It took them eight weeks to complete the process.

The time had come for their skills to be put to the real test. Allen had developed the simulator for the Altair 8800 and Gates had developed the code for the BASIC program. If either failed to work, their whole project would come to nought. Allen took their interpreter to Albuquerque, New Mexico, where MITS was located. He was asked to demonstrate their program in the Altair developed by the company. To his immense relief, it worked successfully. They had managed to develop the software for a machine they hadn't even seen. MITS was satisfied with their work and immediately struck a deal with them. The company bought the rights to distribute their program. The interpreter was named

Altair BASIC. There was no more confusion in Gates's mind. He knew that the software industry would grow by leaps and bounds.

It was the right time to make a decision. His parents supported him when he left Harvard University and joined Allen. In November 1975, they established their first office in Albuquerque and named their company Microsoft. Thus Altair BASIC became the first product developed by Microsoft.

It is believed that Gates first used the name Microsoft in a letter he wrote to Allen on 29 November 1975. The name was a blend of the two words, microcomputer and software.

Initially it was spelt 'Micro-soft', but the hyphen was later dropped. The name was registered as a trademark the following year on 26 November. The Altair BASIC became very popular with personal computer hobbyists. Soon Gates discovered that several copies of their BASIC were illegally circulating in the market. Gates wrote an *Open Letter to Hobbyists* in the *Homebrew Computer Club* newsletter on 3 February 1976. He said, 'Without good software and an owner who understands programming, a hobby computer is wasted. Will quality software be written for the hobby market?'[2]. He explained how much time, money and hard work went into developing the program. All their efforts would go waste if software was not paid for.

By the end of 1976, Microsoft began to develop software for companies other than MITS. On 1 November 1978, its first international office opened in Japan. Named ASCII Microsoft. (ASCII stands for American Standard Code for Information Interchange), it is now called Microsoft Japan. Gates and Allen had established their company in Albuquerque as their first customer, MITS was situated there. Selling it in 1977, they decided by 1979 to shift to a suitable place where they could expand their operations. Though they considered Silicon Valley, they eventually chose Bellevue in Washington State. On 1 January 1979, Microsoft began functioning from its new office in Bellevue.

Microsoft was still in the early stages of its development, with some thirty employees on its payroll. During this period, Gates was involved in all the aspects of the company. He went through each line of every code written. That year, the company's revenues were about 2.4 million dollars. Gates was thinking of ways to boost its growth. One person came to his mind—Steve Ballmer. In Harvard, Gates had become friends with Ballmer, who lived down the hall from him.

Ballmer had graduated in mathematics and economics. He had joined the Stanford University Graduate School of Business. Gates induced him to drop out of Stanford and join him. On 11 June 1980, Ballmer left Stanford and joined Microsoft as its first business manager.

An operating system is a collection of software programs in a computer system. It handles the execution of the various programs and manages storage and other resources in a computer. In 1969, a group of AT&T employees had developed an operating system named UNIX. By the 1980s, different companies, under licence with AT&T, began producing variations of Unix. The operating system developed by Microsoft was also a version of Unix. It was called Xenix. Microsoft released its first operating system in 1980.

Microsoft bought the licence from AT&T in 1979. It intended to develop a version of Unix that would be suitable for use on microcomputers. For this purpose, the task was assigned to Santa Cruz Operations (SCO), a software company that handled Unix porting. Porting is a process in which software is adapted to function in a different environment from the one it was designed originally for. SCO successfully adapted Xenix to the Intel 8086 processor. It purchased the rights from Microsoft to sell the product. Thus, instead of selling it directly to users, Microsoft licensed Xenix to different companies. Subsequently, SCO produced different versions of Xenix. By 1987, Microsoft had ventured into production of a new operating system. Eventually, it sold the complete rights of Xenix to SCO in exchange for owning 25% of SCO.

In 1981, Microsoft struck a deal with the major multinational computer technology firm IBM. Microsoft agreed to develop an operating system for the IBM PC (IBM Personal Computer). This was the first step that catapulted the company into the big league. With the new operating system that it developed for IBM, Microsoft had its first share of success. Its success would soon change the fortune of the company and its founders.

‘Windows’ to the Future

Computers, in the twenty-first century, have connected people in more ways than we could imagine. People all over the world are increasingly becoming Internet-savvy. We often come across words like Microsoft Windows, XP, Apple Mac OS X or Linux in our daily work or home routine.

These are names of some of the leading operating systems in use today. The operating system is the most essential software component in a computer. It coordinates the programs and makes the computer more user-friendly.

Microsoft XP and more recently, Vista, are the latest versions in a long line of operating systems developed by Microsoft, starting in 1980. Their earliest predecessor which helped the company achieve a strong foothold in the industry was MSDOS (Microsoft Disk Operating System). During the 1970s, the most popular operating system used for microcomputers was CP/M (Control Program for Microcomputers). It was developed by Gary Kildall of Digital Research, Inc. Microsoft developed its first hardware product, Microsoft Softcard in 1980. It allowed users to run the CP/M operating system on an Apple II microcomputer.

At that time, IBM was planning to bring out its own line of microcomputers using the Intel 8088 microprocessor. They required a CP/M operating system that would be compatible with the microprocessor. Hence, IBM met Bill Gates with the proposal. When Gates came to know they needed an operating system, he sent them to Digital Research Inc. IBM and Digital Research Inc. had discussions that ended in failure. IBM offered a single license to buy the rights for CP/M and rename it 'PC-DOS'. However, Digital Research was only willing to let IBM use CP/M in exchange for royalties.

When the two companies could not reach an agreement, IBM dropped the offer.

IBM went back to Microsoft with the offer. Their representatives asked Gates to acquire a suitable operating system. Paul Allen knew a programmer who had developed an operating system similar to the CP/M. He was Tim Paterson who worked in a hardware company, Seattle Computer Products (SCP). The company produced computers based on the Intel 8086 microprocessor. They also required an operating system for those computers. The CP/M operating systems available then were not suited to the 8086 microprocessors. Without an operating system, the company was unable to sell its products. Therefore, Paterson started working on a system that would be similar to the CP/M. By July 1980, he had finished the development of QDOS (Quick and Dirty Operating System). The name was soon changed to 86-DOS.

Gates struck a deal with SCP in December 1980. Microsoft bought the licensing rights for 86-DOS. This meant that Microsoft could market it to other hardware manufacturers. Just before the IBM PC was launched on 12 August 1981, Microsoft acquired the complete rights of 86-DOS from SCP. The cost of the whole transaction was around $75,000. Microsoft released it as MS-DOS in 1981. Through an agreement between the two companies, it was decided that both IBM and Microsoft would market their versions of 86-DOS. So, Microsoft could sell MS-DOS to different hardware manufacturers. IBM renamed it PC-DOS and marketed it with the IBM PCs sold through the 1980s and 1990s.

MS-DOS and PC-DOS became extremely popular, but there were initial hiccups for both the companies.

When SCP came to know that Microsoft had licensed 86-DOS to a major company like IBM, it filed a case of fraud against Microsoft. It claimed that Microsoft had not revealed the name of their customer at the time of the agreement. Microsoft settled the case by paying a million dollars to the company in 1986. In the case of IBM, it ran into problems with Digital Research Inc. Digital Research Inc. had discovered that IBM was marketing an operating system that was very similar to their CP/M. Moreover, it had the same name that IBM had suggested during their talks. To avoid any kind of a legal battle, IBM settled to an agreement with Digital Research Inc. According to the agreement, IBM would market both CP/M and PC-DOS with the IBM PCs. The consumer could choose between the two operating systems. However, CP/M was priced at $240, while the PC-DOS cost only $40. The low price of PC-DOS made it a commercial success. Soon, it became the standard for IBM PCs and CP/M eventually was wiped out.

Though PC-DOS was successful, the widespread use of MS-DOS was a result of Gates's business acumen. Before signing the agreement with IBM, Gates managed to retain the copyright of the source code of the operating system. (Source code is a set of instructions written in a programming language that allows the programmer to communicate with the computer.) So IBM never owned the source code of PC-DOS.

Microsoft also had the right to market MS-DOS to various companies.

Initially, there were a number of hardware manufacturers competing with IBM. However, none of them used the Intel 8088 microprocessor. These computers had either MS-DOS or CP/M- 86 as their operating system. IBM PCs had one advantage over the rest of these computers. Its architecture was built in such a way that software ran faster on it than on the other systems. The architecture of a computer is its structural design that outlines the way various components in the system would work. Since IBM was a major manufacturer, most of the software written at the time was designed for it. The other companies realised that there would be greater demand for IBM PCs. As a result, most of the manufacturers began producing computers very similar to the IBM PC. These computers were called PC compatibles or clones.

Around 1983, companies like Columbia Data Products, Eagle Computer and Compaq Computer Corp. released IBM clones. This was an opportunity for MS-DOS to expand its reach. Since Microsoft was not strictly bound only to IBM, it could effectively market MS-DOS to the rest of the companies that were producing PC compatibles. With this move, Microsoft emerged as a key player in the software sector of the home computer industry.

With the success of MS-DOS and PC-DOS, Microsoft and IBM announced the development of OS/2 (Operating System/2). IBM wanted to develop the operating system for the second generation personal computers, PS/2 (Personal System/2). In August 1985, Microsoft signed a Joint Developing Agreement with IBM to develop OS/2. Meanwhile in the same year, on 20 November, Microsoft released the first version of Microsoft Windows. Windows 1.0 was not a complete operating system like MS-DOS. However, it was the first time that Microsoft had used a Graphical User Interface (GUI).

A GUI is a medium that enables users to communicate with an electronic device, like a computer, cell phone or gaming device, through graphical icons instead of textual commands.

The first version of OS/2 was released in December 1985. Through the next few years, various versions of OS/2 and Windows were brought out. Windows 2.0 implemented the Windows version of Microsoft Word and Microsoft Excel for the first time. The terms 'maximise' and 'minimise' also came into use with its release. OS/2 shared a lot of similarities with Windows and also Unix. In the development of OS/2, Microsoft and IBM worked together amicably until

1990. On May 22, 1990, Windows 3.0 was released. The earlier versions had not gained widespread appeal. But Windows 3.0 became immensely popular. When it was released, Windows 3.0 was pre-installed in the new computers. Whereas, OS/2 was sold separately as a high-priced software package. This led to the extensive use of Windows 3.0. More than four million copies of Windows were sold in its first year.[3]

Windows 3.0 became the first version of Windows that was extremely successful for Microsoft. In a single year, Microsoft made revenues of $1.18 billion. This feat made Microsoft the first software company to cross the $1 billion mark in sales in one year.[4]

Microsoft was buoyed by the huge success of Windows 3.0. Soon IBM and Microsoft began to have differences of opinion. It was originally planned that IBM would bring out OS/2 2.0 while Microsoft would be responsible for the development of OS/2 3.0. However, Microsoft was keen to continue investing its time in Windows rather than OS/2. So in May 1991, it decided to hand over the complete responsibility of OS/2 to IBM and concentrate on developing Windows further.

Thereafter, OS/2 was solely developed and maintained by IBM. During the late 1980s, Microsoft also saw significant developments as an organisation. In 1985, it opened its first international production facility in Ireland.

The following year, on 26 February, the company shifted to Redmond in Washington State. A month later, on 13 March, Microsoft brought out its IPO (Initial Public Offering). Throughout the 1990s, Microsoft continued producing subsequent generations of Windows. In the later years, it grew into a multinational corporation and grew in diverse sectors of the software industry. Yet, Windows remains one of the best-selling products in the company's history. Tracking the development of the different versions of Windows also provides an insight into the phenomenal growth of Microsoft.

On the 20 anniversary of Windows, PC Magazine dedicated a whole issue to it. In one of the articles, *Living in a Windows World*, the author, Cade Metz wrote a statement that affirms the universal reach of Windows and the incredible progress of Microsoft, 'Windows is everywhere. Whether you're in a hotel or an airport, a living room or an office, a restaurant or a retail store, it's an odds-on bet that Windows is running on the first PC you see. It's likely running on the servers, too. And, probably the handhelds. Maybe even the cell phones.'[5]

Birth of an Empire

According to 'a leading provider of website statistics for the business market', as of July 2008, Windows holds around 91.02% of the operating systems market.[6] This statistic is a testimony to the complete dominance of Windows in today's world. More than twenty years after the release of Windows 1.0, Microsoft Windows still reigns supreme. Throughout this period, Microsoft managed to put Windows at the top spot with sheer determination and sharp business tactics.

Following the success of Windows 3.0, Microsoft brought out an improved version called Windows 3.1 in 1992. Several extended versions, like Windows for Workgroups, were released in the next one year. These versions were also widely used by corporations. Soon,

IBM and Compaq started selling their PCs which had Windows pre-installed. From being a lesser-known entity, Windows had slowly emerged as the most sought-after operating system. Microsoft's next major release was Windows NT in 1993.

Windows NT was originally supposed to be developed as OS/2 3.0. But differences between IBM and Microsoft led to the break-up of their collaboration. Microsoft hired a software engineer called Dave Cutler to develop NT. In the beginning, it was intended to be an improved version of OS/2. But Dave Cutler developed an entirely different system. NT was not as successful as its predecessors, but has an important place in the Windows family; Windows XP and Vista are based on it.

Relations soured between Microsoft and IBM, and the market witnessed a battle between OS/2 and Windows. As different versions of Windows came out, IBM released subsequent versions of OS/2. However, in 1995, Microsoft scored a victory with the release of Windows 95. With the latest version of Windows, competition from OS/2 was completely thwarted.

Microsoft preceded the launch of Windows 95 with a massive marketing campaign. In fact, it even paid millions of dollars to the band, Rolling Stones, for the rights to use its song, '*Start Me Up*'. The opening chords of the song were played as Gates unveiled the next version of Windows on 24 August 1995. In New York, the Empire State Building was lit up with the trademark colours of Microsoft-red, yellow and green. Later, as Bill Gates addressed the media, the event was broadcast in forty cities around the world. Fortunately for Microsoft, Windows 95 managed to live up to expectations.

Windows 95 was a substantial improvement over Windows 3.1. It differed from its previous versions in one important aspect. The earlier versions were not complete operating systems. They were called 'operating environments' which meant that they had to be used along with MS-DOS.

However, Windows 95 was a complete operating system. This helped in the huge sales, which exceeded those of Windows 3.1. A million copies were sold within four days of its release.

Apart from this, Windows 95 also implemented a variety of new applications. A number of the standard features we see today were used first in it. Some of them include the 'Start' button, the taskbar and the drag-and-drop icons. The 'Start' button enables the user to access different applications. Till the release of Windows Vista, the word 'Start' appeared on the desktop. However, in the latest versions of Windows, it has been replaced by the logo of Microsoft. The taskbar manages the different applications running on the computer at any given time. The drag-and-drop concept allows the user to move files, icons or any other object with the help of the mouse.

Another application that had its origin in Windows 95 was Windows Explorer. It was a kind of file manager that had a graphical user interface (GUI). It allowed the user to access and manipulate different file systems on the computer. By using Windows Explorer, the user could view the contents in each folder. For example, when the user clicks on the 'Documents' icon on the desktop, Windows Explorer opens a new window displaying the contents in the 'Documents' folder. With the help of these kind of applications and other networking improvements, Microsoft made Windows 95 more user-friendly.

Simultaneously with the release of Windows 95, two significant products were also launched by Microsoft. The first one was the Microsoft Network (MSN). It was introduced on the same day as Windows 95. At that time, it was primarily an Internet service provider. Today, MSN includes a plethora of online services provided by Microsoft. The original version of MSN was later named MSN Classic. It was developed by the Advanced Technology Group at Microsoft. It was available along with the other applications in Windows 95. It was an Internet dial-up service. A dial-up service provider enables Internet access with the help of telephone lines. The dial-up service provided by MSN is now second only to AOL (America Online) which has 10 million subscribers in the US and Canada. Later versions of MSN tried to allow easier Internet access to users. However, the focus of attention gradually shifted to the Internet portal, msn.com.

The Internet portal initially began as a platform to promote MSN. Apart from msn.com, Microsoft also hosted two other portals, Microsoft Internet Start and msnbc.com. Microsoft Internet Start was used as a home page that displayed current information and also provided links to different websites. (A home page is the first or main page in a website.) MSNBC and msnbc.com were launched together in 1996. MSNBC was a 24-hours television news channel. It was a tie-up between Microsoft and NBC, a media conglomerate. msnbc.com was the online news provider. NBC has the major share in the television channel but the website is jointly owned by both the companies. The news website has become an established source for quality journalism. In a survey conducted by Nielsen/Net Ratings in June 2008, the website topped the list of Current Events and Global News Sites with 37.6 million users in a month.[7]

Microsoft started to concentrate on msn.com around 1998. The Internet portal underwent several changes and was given a new appearance. The original Microsoft

Internet Start was merged into msn.com. The renovated portal offered news and entertainment content. It hosted different websites belonging to Microsoft. It also provided services like Hotmail, Messenger and MSN Search.

With these features, msn.com soon rivalled popular portals like Yahoo and America Online. Hotmail was a free web mail service originally developed by Jack Smith and Sabeer Bhatia in 1996. It was one of the first free e-mail services, and millions of subscribers used it. A year later, Microsoft, in a major business move, bought Hotmail for nearly $400 million.[8] Since then, Hotmail has been an integral part of Microsoft's web services. In recent times, with competition from Google, Microsoft has revamped its email service. The newest version, named Windows Live Hotmail, was launched in May 2007.

MSN Messenger and MSN Search were launched in 1999. MSN Messenger is a free instant messaging service that allows users to communicate with other users. MSN Search is Microsoft's search engine. A search engine searches for and displays information in response to users' queries. In 2005, Microsoft announced a new product, Windows Live that would comprise most of the web services hosted by the company. Thus, Messenger and Search were renamed Windows Live Messenger and

Windows Live Search respectively. The product also included Windows Live Hotmail.

Windows Live covers communication, sharing, anywhere access and safety.

The second product that came out in the same period as MSN was Windows Internet Explorer, commonly known as IE. The Internet Explorer is a software application known as a web browser. A web browser helps the user to interact with textual or visual information available on a web page in a website. Internet Explorer was developed from the source code of Spyglass Mosaic. Mosaic was a web browser created by Spyglass Inc., an Internet software company. Microsoft struck a deal with the company. According to the agreement, Spyglass licensed Mosaic to Microsoft for a quarterly fee along with royalties obtained from Internet Explorer sales.

The first version was marketed separately from Windows 95. It appeared on an additional product named Microsoft Plus. Hence, it was not available to all the users of the operating system. In the following year, Microsoft released Internet Explorer 3.0.This time around, it was bundled together with the operating system, Windows 95 OSR-1 (a new edition of Windows 95).As a result, it was being provided free to the consumers. Hence, Microsoft did not have to pay royalties thereafter. When Spyglass Inc. threatened to sue the company, Microsoft made a settlement for $8 million. In the development of IE 3.0, Microsoft had not used the Spyglass source code but had used its technology.

Hence, in this and all the later versions till 2006, Spyglass was credited as the licensor of the code for Internet Explorer. The iconic 'e' logo of Internet Explorer first appeared in IE 3.0. IE 3.0 was also successful compared to its previous versions. For the first time, Microsoft was able to compete with the more popular web browser, Netscape Navigator. The market share of Microsoft in the browser market increased. Internet Explorer had now become a serious threat to the other browsers. By the next release of Internet Explorer 4.0, the browser market witnessed the beginning of the 'Browser Wars' between Microsoft and Netscape. Eric Sink, who worked in Spyglass Inc. during that period, wrote in his '*Memoirs From the Browser Wars*', 'We sold our browser technology to 120 companies, but one of them slaughtered the other 119.'[9]

In the next few years, Internet Explorer became the most dominant web browser. With the release of IE 5.0, Microsoft's market share sky-rocketed. By the year 2004, the popularity of Internet Explorer had reached its zenith. That year, nearly 95% of visitors of the Web used it as compared to a meagre percentage who used Netscape Navigator. Since that period, however, it has seen a gradual decline. Though Netscape is no longer a major player, Microsoft has a new rival in Mozilla Firefox. Internet Explorer still remains the most widely used web browser and one of the numerous successes in the history of Microsoft.

Subsequent to Windows 95, Microsoft released consecutive versions—Windows 98, Windows 2000, Windows Millennium Edition (also in 2000), Windows XP (XP standing for eXPerience) in 2001 and Windows Vista in 2007. Microsoft consistently maintained its position in the operating systems market. Most of the later versions met with praise as well as criticism. However, Windows 95 remains the turning point in Microsoft's history. In an interview to PC Magazine, Bill Gates summed up the journey of Windows, 'It went from 'Windows is a joke, who needs it, it's slow' to 'Well, of course we're using Windows, are you kidding me, let's move on to the next topic.' I'm not sure we achieved ultimate mainstream until the shipment of Windows 95.'[10]

Excelling at 'Office' with 'Word'

Windows, Internet Explorer and MSN were products that transformed Microsoft into a multinational computer technology corporation. But Microsoft had its roots in software development. It retained its supremacy in that category owing to its best-selling products like Word, Excel and PowerPoint. These applications have been and still are widely used both in the business and home computers markets.

In 1984, Bill Gates believed that the Apple Macintosh (Mac) was the only microcomputer other than the IBM PC that was worthy of having software written for it. Soon, Microsoft developed two applications that ran on the PCs and later on the Mac. They were Microsoft Word and Microsoft Excel. MS Word is a word processor while

Excel is a spreadsheet application. A word processor is a program that helps in composing, editing and formatting of a text. A spreadsheet is an application that consists of numerous grids of rows and columns. It is generally used to organise numerical data and perform calculations.

Word was initially developed under the name, Multi-Tool Word. It was based on an earlier word processor, Bravo, created by Charles Simonyi when he was working for Xerox Palo Alto Research Center. In 1981, Simonyi left Xerox to join Microsoft. Here, he headed the team responsible for the development of Word and Excel. The name of the application was changed from Multi-Tool Word to Microsoft Word. When it was released in late 1983, it was marketed in a unique way. *PC World*, a computing magazine, carried free copies of Word in its November issue. In the early 1980s, the word processors that were popularly in use were WordStar and WordPerfect. The first version of Microsoft Word failed to evoke a good response from users.

Microsoft Word offered certain features that appeared for the first time in a word processor. Among these was the concept of WYSIWYG (What You See Is What You Get), introduction of line breaks and display of Bold and Italics on the screen. In computer terminology, WYSIWYG implies that what appears on the computer screen is how the text would appear finally. So, as the user writes a document and makes any changes, he would be able to conceive the end-result. Additionally, as features like Bold and Italics were included, the user could implement these directly. Earlier, when WYSIWYG was not available, the user had to type specific commands to direct the computer to make necessary changes. Even the margins and spacing were not displayed in the document. With the invention of WYSIWYG, the editing and composition of the text became easier. Microsoft Word also had a special character that indicated the beginning of a new line. This is called a line break or newline.

In spite of these features, Word was not used by major companies. The reason was that Word also had some deficiencies. The application required extensive use of the mouse, which at that time was not a normal practice. It also employed certain complicated procedures even for a simple task like saving a file. Most users had already become familiar with WordPerfect. Hence, they did not find the necessity to get acquainted to newer software.

Microsoft Word was also developed for the Apple Mac microcomputer in 1985. This time around, more features were added to enhance WYSIWYG effect. This helped in increasing the sales of Word. As Microsoft continued bringing out versions of Word, the market was still dominated by WordPerfect. The trend changed in the year 1989. Microsoft had shifted its focus from DOS to Windows by that time. It released its first version of Word for Windows in November 1989.

This was a crucial moment in deciding the future of the word processors. Windows was slowly emerging as the dominant operating system. Hence, Microsoft Word saw a considerable hike in its market share. WordPerfect made a fatal mistake by not developing a version for Windows immediately. By the time Windows 3.0 was released in 1990, Microsoft Word had become the leader in word processors. Though WordPerfect released its version for Windows in 1991, it was too late. Word designed for Windows was a superior product and more importantly, it came into the market earlier.

In later years, Microsoft Word has been developed for the IBM PC, the Apple Macintosh, Windows and SCO Unix. Word now has competitors like OpenOffice.org Writer and Google Docs. But it still remains the most commonly used word processor in the market.

Microsoft Excel was planned and developed at the same time as Word. In 1984, Microsoft decided to launch a spreadsheet application, Multiplan that would increase efficiency in handling numerical data. It was developed for CP/M as well as MS-DOS. It performed well on CP/M but faced tough competition for MS-DOS. For the DOS operating systems, the spreadsheet application that was in demand was Lotus 1-2-3. It was also a spreadsheet program developed by Lotus Software (which was later acquired by IBM). It was released in 1983 and was notable for its speed and user-friendliness.

Microsoft then decided to relaunch Multiplan as Microsoft Excel for the Mac in 1985. Excel used the graphical user interface (GUI) that made it easier to use. Thus the user could manipulate the appearance of the spreadsheet. It was later bundled with Windows in 1987. In fact, it was one of the first applications that was launched for Windows. Meanwhile, Lotus 1-2-3 continued its versions for OS/2 for IBM. This proved to be the deciding factor in Excel's favour. Lotus 1-2-3 was not available for Windows. With the rising popularity of Windows, Excel managed to amass a higher number of users. It was a matter of few years for Excel to become the leading spreadsheet program.

The other application that defines the range of Microsoft's products is Microsoft PowerPoint. Commonly used in businesses and education, PowerPoint is a presentation program. The original creators of PowerPoint were Bob Gaskin and Dennis Austin. Together they had developed a program named Presenter for their company, Forethought in 1984. The name was later changed to PowerPoint. The first version was released in 1987. It was developed for the Apple Macintosh. The pages in the initial version appeared only in black-and-white. The same year, Microsoft bought both the company and its product, PowerPoint for $14 million.[11] A year later, PowerPoint was available in its full-colour version.

PowerPoint is an extremely useful tool in any sort of presentation. The application enables the consecutive use of a number of pages or slides. The process is somewhat similar to a slide projector, used to display photographic images. These slides can be used to convey ideas through textual or visual content. With the help of a video projector, presentations can be made for meetings or conferences having more number of viewers. Microsoft released its version for Windows in 1990.

Within three years, PowerPoint had captured a major share of the presentation market. Since then, PowerPoint has made things a lot easier for everyone who has had to make a presentation. By 2001, it was estimated that at least thirty million PowerPoint presentations were made in a single day.[12] It had completely dominated the presentation-software market. Nowadays, it's not only used for business, technical or educational purposes but also for general everyday occasions.

In an article, *Absolute Powerpoin*' in the May 2001 issue of the *New Yorker*, Ian Power narrated the following incident. A few years earlier, Bob Gaskin attended a conference in Britain that had a number of presentations. At one point, the conference was stopped as the organiser announced,

'I've just been told that the inventor of PowerPoint is in the audience. Will he please identify himself so we can recognise his contribution to the advancement of science?' Gaskin stood up to tremendous applause. Indeed, PowerPoint has revolutionised the method of conveying information.

These three applications—Word, Excel and PowerPoint—were bundled together as Microsoft Office in 1989. For the first time, Office was released for the Apple Mac. In 1990, it was produced for Windows. Microsoft Office is a software suite, which is a collection of application software. Since it is designed for use in the workplace, it is often called an office suite. Microsoft Office thus was a comprehensive tool offering a word processor, a spreadsheet program and a presentation program. With the consequent releases of Windows versions, Office was upgraded with several additions. It is available both for Windows and the Apple Mac computers. The Office suite now is an expansive set of programs that covers all the aspects necessary for businesses.

Some of the applications of Office are—Outlook, a corporate e-mail service that also helps the user in maintaining and organising personal information; Visio, a drawing and diagramming program that helps in visualising and communicating complex information; Communicator, that enables interaction between people in different locations and time zones; and Publisher, which helps in creating publishing or marketing material.

Having captured the operating systems market with Windows, Microsoft did the same with its application software. In fact, it is believed that the applications helped in the immense popularity of Windows. Often referred to as 'killer apps', Word, Excel and PowerPoint drove most of their famed predecessors out of competition. (A killer application or 'killer app' in computer terminology is a program that is revolutionary and popular). A majority of offices around the world today make use of Microsoft Office Suite. Reports claim that there are anywhere between 400 to 600 million users of Microsoft Office worldwide.[13]

More than thirty years after its humble beginnings in Albuquerque, Microsoft has emerged as the single-most dominant player in the software industry. Offering world-class products and determined to maintain its leading position, the company has become an icon of brilliance, thanks to the visionary genius of Bill Gates.

Workings of a Great Mind

In 2008, Bill Gates was ranked third in the *Forbes* list of billionaires in the world with a net worth of $58 billion. But this was only after thirteen years of reigning at the top.[14]

When he first crossed the billion mark in 1987, he was the youngest self-made billionaire. Microsoft's surge in the software industry made Bill Gates the most influential, wealthiest and most recognised individual in the business world. Conversely, the sheer dominance of Microsoft can be attributed to the talent, dedication and business acumen of Gates.

Microsoft was founded by Gates and Allen. Allen had played a key role in the early years of the company. However, in 1983, during a trip to Europe, Allen was diagnosed with Hodgkin's Disease. Post-treatment, Allen chose not to return to Microsoft. Instead, he devoted his time to his new company, Asymetrix Inc. In 2000, Allen also officially stepped down from re-election to Microsoft's board of directors, but retained his ties by accepting the role of senior strategy advisor.

After Allen's exit, Gates became responsible for the major decisions that Microsoft took. Throughout its history, Gates has been the force behind software development, business strategies and every crucial decision made. He hired the best knowledge workers. He established a great working environment that rewarded merit and efficiency. He fiercely defended every step the company took. Before officially retiring from his executive duties, he was quoted as saying, 'We've really achieved the ideal of what I wanted Microsoft to become.' [15]

From MS-DOS to Windows to Microsoft Office, Gates has shown creativity, intellectual ability and insight into trade and commerce. His vision was to create cost-effective, superior and advanced software that would make computing an enjoyable experience. Right from the beginning, Gates made accurate decisions in hiring the right people to achieve his goals.

Examples are his appointment of Steve Ballmer, who headed several divisions before succeeding Gates as the CEO; the deal with Seattle Computer Products for

QDOS and the hiring of its creator, Tim Paterson; the hiring of Charles Simonyi to develop Microsoft Word; the purchase of the company Forethought and its product, PowerPoint; the licensing of the source code for Internet Explorer from Spyglass Inc. These noteworthy decisions steered Microsoft towards success.

Some of the choices made by Gates proved to be turning points in the company's history.

Beginning with MS-DOS, Gates persuaded IBM to allow Microsoft to market it to other companies. This decision paved the way for the popularity of MS-DOS. Later with the success of Windows, Gates began to concentrate more on it than OS/2. This resulted in the complete dominance of Windows in the operating systems market. Jeff Raikes was the director of Applications Marketing in 1984. When he proposed the bundling of applications into Microsoft Office, Gates supported his suggestion. Office became one of Microsoft's best-selling software products. In 1995, Gates recognised the importance of Internet. Microsoft developed Internet Explorer, which drove Netscape out of contention.

In 1994, Gates started the initiative to gather new ideas in an innovative concept called Think Week. Every year, for one week, he would take off to a remote and secluded place in Northwest America. During this week, away from family and colleagues, Gates read papers written by his employees. Weeks earlier, the employees prepared to draft their views and concerns. They were encouraged to discuss the issues related to the company. This concept also allowed them to voice their ideas regarding the future of technology. Gates read more than a hundred papers in that week. On an average, he spent up to 18 hours a day, reading and commenting. By 2006, the process had become digital and open to the whole company.

Gates's management style has evoked both praise and criticism. Microsoft spent considerable time and money in recruiting new and young software talent. These software developers occupied a prime position in the company. But they had to live up to Gates's expectations. Often in presentations and meetings, executives were subjected to tough challenges posed by Gates. It is believed that he often used the phrase, 'the stupidest thing I've ever heard'.[16]Often criticised for this tough approach, he claimed in his defence that he criticised not the people but their ideas. He believed that conflict was an effective way of exploiting potential. At the same time, he appreciated an employee who stood up to his challenges. Esther Dyson, a journalist and technology investor, who knew Gates well, once observed, 'I always felt with Bill, if he bothered to argue with you, it was a sign of respect. If he didn't bother to engage, that's when you needed to really worry.'[17]

In meetings, it was described that he would close his eyes and rock back and forth. His attention would never wander as he relentlessly posed questions. Employees regarded his attitude positively. They had to be completely confident of their presentation and be prepared for any scrutiny.

Some of them had pleasant memories of their interaction with Gates. One of the general managers at Microsoft, Tandy Trower, remembered receiving encouraging advice from Gates in his initial years. He remarked, 'I can remember from the very early days at Microsoft how inspiring Bill was—not just because he was a smart guy, but because of the things he would do on a personal level.'[18]

Controversies have also surrounded Microsoft's business strategies. The company had its share of litigation and lawsuits. Criticism was levelled at the aggressive business tactics employed by Gates. Most of his competitors believed that Gates was responsible for the monopolisation of the software market. Microsoft had completely dominated the operating systems, the web browser and the software applications markets. A common accusation was that this monopoly had stifled creativity and curbed innovation.

In 1998, the United States Department of Justice (DOJ) filed an antitrust suit against Microsoft Corporation.

The issue was whether Microsoft could be allowed to bundle Internet Explorer with Windows for free. The complainants believed that the company had monopolised the sales of operating systems and web browsers. After a lengthy court procedure, the case was finally settled in 2001. It required Microsoft to share certain software information with third-party companies.

During this period, Gates made his stand clear. In a corporate e-mail, he fervently expressed the reasons for the decisions he made for the company. He believed that Microsoft had achieved superiority because of a fiercely competitive environment. Elaborating on the need for innovation, he explained that the company strove to create software that would make the personal computer available and easy-to-use for everyone. By bundling Internet Explorer with Windows, he felt that the company had responded to consumers' needs. He thought that the case was a move by rivals who could not compete with Microsoft. If it succeeded, he believed that the intervention would prevent innovation and creativity.

Though Gates has earned many enemies with his business tactics, a vast majority also acknowledges his contribution. Many believe that Windows played a significant role in the development of the computer industry. It provided a standard on which thousands of software and hardware companies could innovate. No one can deny the fact that Gates revolutionised the PC industry.

As Gates stepped down from his executive duties and ventured into philanthropy, the transition marked the end of an era in the history of software technology.

From Software to Service

On 1 January 1994, Bill Gates married a former employee, Melinda French. They have three children—Jennifer Katherine Gates, Rory John Gates and Phoebe Adele Gates. They live in a massive lakeside home in Washington. Gates owns a library consisting of rare books, including the writings of Leonardo da Vinci. Despite being one of the richest men in the world, he remains grounded. He prefers to fly in business class only in Europe. He always travels by coach in the United States. His interests include reading, solving puzzles and playing golf.

The *Time* magazine once quoted Gates as saying that he wished he were not the richest man in the world. He felt that this fact attracted attention he disliked. He was greatly influenced by Warren Buffet, an American investor and philanthropist. Buffet, the CEO of Berkshire Hathaway, was ranked first in the *Forbes* list of billionaires in February 2008. He is known for his simple lifestyle and charitable work.

Gates met Buffet on 5 July 1991. It was an experience that would change the way he thought and worked. Inspired by Buffet, Gates and his wife started the Bill & Melinda Gates Foundation in 2000. Based in Seattle, Washington, the Foundation was initially funded by Gates. It is headed by Bill, Melinda and William Gates Sr. The CEO Patty Stonesifer was recently succeeded by Jeff Raikes. In 2006, Buffet donated a major portion of his fortune to the Foundation. This made it one of the wealthiest private foundations. The foundation differs from most charities in its transparency. The details of all the grants made by it are published.

Before their marriage, Bill's mother Mary Gates wrote to Melinda, 'From those to whom much is given, much is expected.'[19] This was the inspiration for their commitment to philanthropy. It also led to the principle behind the foundation's work—a belief that every life had equal value. The foundation aims at improving healthcare and reducing poverty. In the United States, it plans to give those in need equal opportunities for education and access to technology. The foundation has been divided into three programmes for global development, global health and the United States.

The Global Development Program deals with three key issues—agricultural development, financial services for the poor and global libraries. As most of the poverty-stricken people depend on agriculture, the Foundation provides tools to improve productivity. For the supply of funds, it offers financial help. As information is essential, it supports free access to computers.

The Global Health Program has two priorities—access to vaccines, medicines or tools to combat diseases; and funding research to develop effective and affordable preventive measures. The Foundation has undertaken several initiatives in this program. One of them has been the establishment of Avahan in India. Avahan aims at preventing the spread of AIDS in the most-affected states in the country.

The United States Program is divided into—education, the Pacific Northwest and US Libraries. The Foundation believes that every child has the right to get educated and graduate from high school. It offers students scholarships to pursue their goals. In the Pacific Northwest (the Washington State and neighbouring region of Greater Portland, Oregon), low-income families are given support for housing and other basic needs. The libraries in the United States are a major resource for free access to computers and the Internet. Therefore, the foundation ensures that these libraries are equipped with the necessary quality technology.

In 2005, *Time* magazine recognised Bill and Melinda Gates for their charitable work. Along with singer Bono, it named them Persons of the Year 2005. In May 2006, the Prince of Asturias annual awards in Spain honoured the foundation for International Cooperation. A few months later, the foundation was split into two organisations. Bill & Melinda Gates Foundation Trust handled the donation of money or property made to the foundation. The other entity, Bill & Melinda Gates Foundation managed the operations and allocation of grants.

In 2008, Gates moved from his full-time position in Microsoft to full-time work at the foundation. Many have appreciated and praised the decision. They believe that Gates will direct his aggressive tactics in competing not against rivals but maladies affecting society. By devoting his energies to the foundation, they feel he will be able to bring a great difference to its strategy.

Being an influential figure, Gates hopes to engage in discussions at the highest levels of government and industry.

He plans to spend one day at the Redmond office, two days at the foundation and two at his personal office in a week. As part of his work for the foundation, he aims to read extensively about education and science. His primary focus is on AIDS and malaria. He realises that the issues he has to deal with now are more serious than his work at Microsoft. He is prepared to serve the foundation with the same amount of dedication and passion as he did with software. People who know him well believe that his presence will make a definite impact. Warren Buffet said, 'He'll be competing with his own standards. In the end, he is going to want people to look at the Gates Foundation 100 years from now and say, 'This guy did it the way it should have been done.'[20]

The Remarkable Life of an Icon

Entrepreneur, billionaire, software guru, astute businessman, brilliant leader, philanthropist—Bill Gates has played every role to perfection. His journey, from being a young programmer to becoming chairman of a huge corporation, has been glorious and eventful. In his career, the highs have significantly prevailed over the lows.

Gates has received overwhelming recognition for his efforts in the development of software technology. In 1999, *Time* magazine published a list of a hundred people who had influenced the 20 century. Gates was among the four people who appeared in the first list and also the second one, published in 2004. The second list compiled the hundred people who continue to have an influence on the world. Since 2004, the list has become an annual feature. Gates figured in the list again in 2005 and 2006.

Gates has appeared in several lists similar to the *Time* magazine list. Universities around the world awarded him doctorates. In a survey conducted in 1999, he was ranked the second most powerful person in Britain, after Prime Minister Tony Blair.[21] Queen Elizabeth II bestowed the honour of Knight Commander of the Order of the British Empire (KBE) on him in 2005.[22] Interestingly, a flower fly has been named *Eristalis gatesi*, in 'recognition of his great contributions to the science of Dipterology'.[23] Gates has also authored two books—*The Road Ahead* in 1995 and *Business @ the Speed of Thought* in 1999.

The success of his company can be attributed to Gates's passion for his work. On 22 June, 2008, *Newsweek* published an interview with Gates quoting his words in the headline, 'There's no year that I didn't love my job'.[24]

At fifty-two, with a string of accomplishments behind him, he seeks to attain the higher goal of giving back to the world. The future will decide his success in his philanthropic endeavours. But irrespective of the outcome, one fact remains undeniable—as a legend, the name of Bill Gates will be etched in history forever.